2's Fingerplays EXPERIENCE

by
Liz & Dick Wilmes

Illustrations by
Janet McDonnell

A  Publication

38W567 Brindlewood, Elgin, Illinois   60123

ISBN 0-943452-18-X

ART

Cover Design and Graphics:	David VanDelinder STUDIO 155 Elgin, Illinois 60123
Computer Graphics:	Arlene Fiebig PAPER PUSHERS Fontana, Wisconsin 53125
Text Graphics:	Janet McDonnell Early Childhood Artist Arlington Heights, Illinois 60004

SPECIAL THANKS TO:

Cheryl Luppino and Mary Steinman for sharing many of the fingerplays and games they play with their toddlers and twos along with the techniques they use to make each one appropriate, fun, and exciting.

PUBLISHED BY:
  BUILDING BLOCKS
  38W567 Brindlewood
  Elgin, Illinois 60123

ISBN 0-943452-18-X

Contents

Planes, Trains & More

Self

Our Bodies

Our Bodies (cont.)

Rest & Relax

Farm Animals

Zoo Animals

Forest Animals

Bugs & Insects

Appendix

INTRODUCTION

When Doing Fingerplays With Toddlers and Twos

● Laugh a lot.

● Clap during and/or after each one.

● Repeat often.

● Do the movements with the children.

● Encourage, but never force, everyone to participate.

● Use props when appropriate:

  ✓ Velcro® glove
  ✓ Felt board pieces
  ✓ Real objects
  ✓ Equipment
  ✓ Furniture

● Talk and sing slowly so that children have time to move.

● Animate your voices to portray the different characters.

● Exaggerate your movements.

● Use the FINGERPLAY CARDS

  ✓ Lay several CARDS on the floor for the children to see.
  ✓ Let the children choose one.
  ✓ Pick it up and hold it as you say the rhyme.
  ✓ Use the words on the back if you wish.
  ✓ Choose another card and enjoy another fingerplay.

Make FINGERPLAY CARDS

You'll Need

Construction paper
Clear adhesive paper or laminate
Scissors
White glue or spray glue

To Make Each CARD: If you're using white glue, water it down slightly. Cut the construction paper into a 51/2" square.

Brush or spray glue onto the backside of the Fingerplay Illustration and adhere it to oneside of the CARD. Apply glue to the backside of the Words/Movement and place it on the second side of the CARD. Let it dry. Laminate the CARD or cover both sides of it with clear adhesive paper.

front side

back side

clear adhesive

Make a Simple Velcro® Glove and Pieces

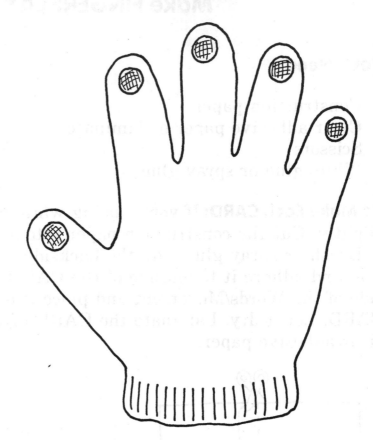

You'll Need
- Work glove
- Velcro® dots
- Figures or objects for the glove

To Make Your Glove:
Wash you work glove. Fasten one side of a Velcro® dots to each finger/thumb of the glove. For additional strength, sew the dots to the fingers/thumb.

To Make the Pieces: Gather the objects or duplicate, color, and cut out the pictures. Fasten the opposite side of a Velcro® dot to the backside of each piece.

Store Your Pieces

You'll Need
- Large envelops or large resealable plastic bags
- Permanent marker

To Store: Place each FINGERPLAY CARD along with the appropriate pieces in an individual envelop/bag. On the outside of it write the name of the fingerplay and list of the pieces. Place all of the envelops/bags in an easily available storage bin.

March & Move

FINGER BAND

Help Children:
- **Control rhythm sticks.**
- **March.**

RHYTHM STICK FUN
Give each child a rhythm stick. As you sing each verse *"play your rhythm sticks"* to imitate the appropriate instrument.

VARIATION: March around the room as you sing and *"play your rhythm sticks."*

FINGER BAND
(tune: Here We Go Round the Mulberry Bush)

The finger band is coming to town,
   (Fingers behind back marching slowly to front.)
Coming to town, coming to town.
The finger band is coming to town,
So early in the morning.

This is the way they play their horns...
   (Hands to mouth and blow.)
This is the way they play their drums...
   (Beating motion.)
This is the way they play their flutes...
   (Hands near mouth, wiggle fingers.)

The finger band is going away,
   (Fingers marching behind back.)
Going away, going away.
The finger band is going away,
So early in the morning.

JACK BE NIMBLE

Help Children:
- Anticipate.
- Jump up and down.
- Jump over an object.

JUMP OVER
Cut a one foot piece of heavy yarn or string for each child to use as a candle.

Give everyone a piece of yarn or string. Put the *candles* on the floor near your feet. Say the rhyme and jump over your *candles* as you say, *"Jack jump over the candlestick."*

VARIATION: Play this game with several children or an individual child. Change the name in the rhyme to the child's name. The child jumps over the *candlestick* when the rhyme directs. (If a child needs help, hold his hand as he is jumping.)

JACK BE NIMBLE

Jack be nimble.

Jack be quick.

Jack jump
   (Jump up and down.)

Over the candlestick.

JACK-IN-THE-BOX

IN THE BOX

Get cardboard boxes large enough for individual children to sit in.

Let the children get in the boxes or squat with their hands covering their heads. Say the rhyme while sitting very still. At the end everyone jump up and out of the box.

JACK IN THE BOX

Jack in the box.
(Hide thumb in fist.)

Sits so still.

Won't you come out?

Yes I will.
(Pop thumb out of fist.)

JOHNNY WORKS

Help Children:
- **Count.**
- **Control rhythm sticks.**

RHYTHM STICK FUN
Give everyone rhythm sticks. Pound the floor with one stick as you sing, *"Johnny works with one hammer..."* and two sticks as you sing, *"Johnny works with two hammers..."* Continue pounding with the sticks as you add your legs and head to the song. At the end stop all of the hammers and everyone lie down on the floor to rest. Tiptoe around the resting children and pick up the rhythm sticks or wake-up and play again!

JOHNNY WORKS WITH ONE HAMMER

Johnny works with one hammer,
   (Pound 1 fist.)
One hammer, one hammer.
Johnny works with one hammer,
All day long.

Johnny works with two hammers...
   (Pound 2 fists.)

Johnny works with three hammers...
   (Pound 2 fists, 1 leg.)

Johnny works with four hammers...
   (Pound 2 fists, 2 legs.)

Johnny works with five hammers...
   (Pound 2 fists, 2 legs, head.)

Now he goes to sleep.
   (Whisper and lie down.)

LONDON BRIDGE

Help Children:
- Play a group game.
- Sing and move.
- Anticipate.

IN PAIRS

Pair up with a child and make the *London Bridge* together. Sing as you're holding it up. As you sing the third line, fall down. Clap for each other.

BALANCE BOARD

Put a long, wide board or piece of tape on the floor. Pretend that it is a bridge. Have a bucket of small vehicles. Let the children *drive* them along the bridge.

LONDON BRIDGE

London Bridge is falling down,
   (Make a bridge with a child.)

Falling down, falling down.
   (All children go under the bridge.)

London Bridge is falling down.

My fair lady/gentleman.
   (Catch, hug, and release last child going under bridge.)

Sing over and over again as children continue going under the bridge.

MARCHING WE WILL GO

Help Children:
- **March.**
- **Transition.**

GATHER UP

When it is time to transition to another activity such as outdoors, lunch, etc. gather up the children by slowly marching around the room and singing *Marching We Will Go.* Encourage the children to join you.

After you have sung the verse several times keep marching and gathering up the children but change the words to signal where you are going. For example:

- *Outside we will go...*
- *Lunch we will go...*
- *Naptime we will go...*
(Quietly marching.)

VARIATION: March and sing with one child as you and he are going someplace such as:

- *Easel we will go...*
- *Table we will go...*
- *Rocker we will go...*

MARCHING WE WILL GO
(tune: Farmer In the Dell)

A marching we will go.
   (March in place.)

A marching we will go.

Hi-ho the derry-oh.

A marching we will go.

MR/MS CLOWN

DO A TRICK

Sit in a circle. Name a child to be the clown in the middle. Chant the fingerplay and clap to the rhythm.

After everyone *clicks* his fingers, the clown in the middle does a trick, movement, or exercise. Everyone does what the clown is doing. Clap and then name another clown.

HINT: Some children might want someone in the middle with them. You could ask each clown, *"Do you want me to come into the middle with you?"*

MR/MS CLOWN

Mr/Ms Clown, Mr/Ms Clown
(*Clap hands while chanting.*)

He's/She's the funniest
clown in town.

Click... (*Snap fingers.*)

Do a trick. (*Everyone bow.*)

POP GOES THE WEASEL

Help Children:
- **Practice balance.**
- **Cooperate.**

CIRCLE FUN
Hold hands, slowly walk around in a circle, and sing *Pop Goes The Weasel*. As you are singing, bend lower and lower to the ground as if you're the monkey chasing the weasel. When you sing, *"Pop goes the weasel"* jump up! Clap. Hold hands and play again.

POP GOES THE WEASEL

All around the
            cobbler's bench

The monkey chased
        the weasel,

The monkey thought
        it was all in fun,

Pop!
Goes the weasel.

ROUND THE VILLAGE

Help Children:
- Play group games.
- Cooperate.
- Control a parachute.

PARACHUTE FUN

You'll need a parachute, bedsheet, or tablecloth. Stand around the parachute holding it with two hands. *Warm-up* by waving the chute up and down.

Now turn one direction holding the chute with one hand. After everyone is holding the chute and facing in the same direction, start singing and walking in a circle.

Stop after the first verse. Hold the chute with two hands. Sing the second verse while stepping forward and backward or waving the chute. Stop. Sing the third verse while slowly running.

HINT: If running in a circle is too difficult, hold the chute with two hands and march.

ROUND AND ROUND THE VILLAGE

Walk round and round the village,
  (Join hands and walk in a circle.)
Walk round and round the village,
Walk round and round the village,
As we have done before.

Step in and out the circle...
  (Step forward and backward.)

Run round and round the village...
  (Slowly run in a circle.)

Repeat the first verse while walking.

22

STRETCH

Help Children:
- **Balance.**

TOUCH THE SUN

Get several yellow beachballs and hang them from the ceiling just out of reach of the children.

OR

Have the children make suns for the room. Get several paper grocery bags, put them on the art table, and let the children paint them. Set the bags off to the side to dry. When they are dry, stuff each *sun* with waded up newspaper, and then staple it closed. Hang your *suns* from the ceiling just out of reach of the children. As you are saying *Stretch* try to touch the *suns*.

STRETCH

I stretch and stretch
   (Stretch high.)
And find it fun.
To reach and reach
   (Stretch on tiptoes.)
To touch the sun.

I bend and bend
   (Bend down.)
To touch the floor.
I stand back up
   (Stretch high again.)
And stretch some more.
   (Clap.)

TING-A-LING

CIRCUS TRICKS

Put a tumbling mat/mattress in the middle of the floor. Pretend it is the circus ring. Have the children sit around it. Say the rhyme and name a child. That child does his trick in the *circus ring*. Everyone claps for him. Repeat over and over.

TING-A-LING

I am a circus clown

My name is Ting-A-Ling
(Point to self.)

Let (child's name),

Do a funny trick
(Child does a trick.)

In our circus ring.

24

HUP 2, 3, 4

Help Children:

- Play rhythm instruments.
- March their whole bodies.
- March their hands.
- Count.

MARCHING FEET

Pass out the rhythm instruments. March around the room and chant *Hup 2, 3, 4* while playing the instruments. Stop after awhile, switch instruments, and continue the parade.

VARIATION: March and clap instead of marching and playing rhythm instruments.

MARCHING HANDS

Sit with the children on the floor or at a table. Chant *Hup 2, 3, 4*. As you chant let your *marching hands* keep the beat on your legs, floor, or table.

HINT: You might want to change the last line to, *"We're sitting on the floor."* or *"We're sitting at the table."*

HUP 2, 3, 4

Hup 2, 3, 4
    (March in place.)
Hup 2, 3, 4
Hup 2, 3, 4
Let's march some more.
    (Clap.)

Hup 2, 3, 4
Hup 2, 3, 4
Hup 2, 3, 4
Let's sit on the floor.
    (Sit down.)

HUP 2, 3, 4

HUP 2, 3, 4

Help Children:
- Play rhythm instruments.
- March their whole bodies.
- March their hands.
- Count.

MARCHING FEET
Pass out the rhythm instruments. March around the room and chant Hup 2, 3, 4 while playing the instruments. Stop after awhile, switch instruments and continue the parade.

VARIATION: March and clap instead of marching and playing rhythm instruments.

MARCHING HANDS
Sit with the children...

HUP 2, 3, 4

Hup 2, 3, 4
March together
Hup 2, 3, 4
Hup 2, 3, 4
Let's march together...

Fall Down

APPLE TREE

Help Children:
- Become aware of numbers.
- Stretch their bodies.
- Name foods they like to eat.
- Control rhythm sticks.

UMMMMMM GOOD
Say *Apple Tree* with the children, being certain to exaggerate your voices and s-t-r-e-t-c-h your muscles. Ask the children what other foods they like. After each food is named, repeat, *"Ummmmm! Ummmmm! Good!"* as you rub your tummies.

KEEP THE BEAT
Sit down and pass out the rhythm sticks. Say the rhyme. Point high in the air with the sticks during the first verse and pound the floor with them as you say the second verse.

APPLE TREE

Way up high in the apple tree.
  (Two arms reach high in the air.)
Two little apples smiled at me.
  (Put index fingers to cheeks.)

I shook that tree as hard as I could.
  (Shake tree with two hands.)
Down came the apples.
  (Tap floor.)

Ummmmm! Ummmmm! Good!
  (Rub tummies.)

CLOTHES ON FIRE

Help Children:
- **Learn fire safety.**
- **Roll their bodies.**

STOP, DROP, ROLL
Put a large mat on the floor. Call a child's name. He gets on the mat. Everyone say the rhyme together. As you're saying it, the child stops, drops to the mat, and rolls to the end. (Help him roll if he needs it.) Clap for him and say, *"The fire is out."* Repeat for all of the children to play as often as they would like.

MEET THE FIREFIGHTERS
Call your local fire station. Make an appointment for a firefighter to come and talk with the children about fire prevention and safety.

CLOTHES ON FIRE

Clothes on fire
Don't get scared.

STOP! *(Freeze.)*
DROP! *(Fall to the floor.)*
ROLL! *(Log roll.)*

Dick Wilmes

HUMPTY DUMPTY

HUMPTY PUZZLE

Duplicate and enlarge the pattern to make a giant *Humpty Dumpty*. Color it, glue it to posterboard, and cover it with clear adhesive (laminate). Now cut the giant *Humpty Dumpty* into 3-5 pieces.

Say the rhyme with the children. After saying it spread out the pieces on the floor and put *Humpty Dumpty* back together again. Clap for *Humpty!*

EXTENSION: Put the puzzle on a table for the children to put together again and again.

HUMPTY DUMPTY

Humpty Dumpty sat on a wall.
  (Sit cross-legged.)
Humpty Dumpty had a great fall.
  (Fall over.)

All the king's horses and
    all the king's men.
Couldn't put Humpty
    together again.

But I can!
  (Go and touch each Humpty Dumpty. Children sit back up.)

I'M A LITTLE ACORN

Help Children:
- **Become aware of body position.**
- **Learn about acorns.**

WALK OVER ME
Have the children curl up like acorns. Say the rhyme while *walking over* and *tapping* each acorn. As you crack the acorns have them sit up and start clapping.

ACORN HUNT
If you have acorns in your area, take a basket and go for a walk. Look for acorns along the way. Put them in your basket.

When you get back to the room let each child put one or more acorns in a sandwich bag. Staple a note to each which says, *"We went on an ACORN HUNT today."* Take them home.

I'M A LITTLE ACORN

I'm a little acorn small and round
   (Curl up on floor.)
Lying on the cold, cold ground.
Everyone walks over me,
That is why I'm cracked you see.

I'm a nut! *(Clap, clap.)*

I'm a nut! *(Clap, clap.)*

I'm a nut ! *(Clap, clap.)*

I'M A LITTLE TEAPOT

Help Children:
• **Coordinate their arms and bodies to do different actions.**
• **Name liquids they like to drink.**

TIP ME OVER
Sit with several children on the floor. (You are the cups.) Have other children stand around the cups. (They are the teapots.) Everyone begin to sing. When it's time to pour the tea, have the teapots tip towards the cups and carefully fill them up. Pretend to drink your tea at the end of the song!

VARIATION: Place unbreakable cups on the floor. Everyone be teapots and pour tea into the cups.

EXTENSION: Talk about everyone's favorite drinks. Walk around and fill the teapots (children) with them. Sing the song again with all of the children pouring their favorite drinks into cups. Enjoy drinking the treats.

I'M A LITTLE TEAPOT

I'm a little teapot, short and stout.
Here is my handle,
(One hand on hip.)
Here is my spout.
(Other arm straight out.)

When I get all steamed up,
Hear me shout,
"Tip me over and pour me out."
(Bend to the side.)

I'M A TOP

Help Children:
- **Gain a sense of balance.**

BY MYSELF

Get a mechanical top, pump it up, and let it spin. As you are pumping, chant, *"Pump, pump, pump, ..."* When you let it go, shout out, *"Spin!"*

Ask a child, *"Do you want to be a top?"* Stand next to her and pump her up. Chant as you pump. When she's ready shout, *"Spin!"* The child spins until she wants to fall down. Do again or with other children.

Put the mechanical top on the floor so that the children can play with it.

I'M A TOP

I'm a top all wound up tight.
(Hands around chest.)

I whirl and whirl with all my might.
(Turn around and around.)

And now the whirls are out of me.
(Fall down.)

So I fall down as fast as can be.
(Rest.)

I'M BOUNCING

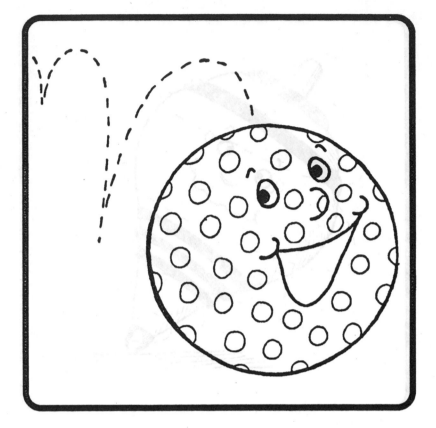

Help Children:
- **Exercise their whole body.**
- **Relax.**

BOUNCE AROUND THE ROOM

Pretend that you are a ball and start bouncing around the room as you say the fingerplay. Encourage the children to bounce with you. At the last line everyone fall down. While on the ground, rest and take several deep breaths.

Before you get up tell the children where you're going to bounce to next, such as the door, book shelf, teddy bear in the rocker, etc. Get up, start saying the rhyme and bouncing to the next spot. Play until you've bounced all around the room.

I'M BOUNCING

I'm bouncing, bouncing, everywhere.
(Jump in place.)

I bounce and bounce into the air.

I'm bouncing, bouncing like a ball.

I bounce and bounce, then down I fall.
(Fall down.)

JACK AND JILL

Help Children:
- **Exercise their whole body.**
- **Climb stairs.**

JUMP WITH JACK AND JILL

Turn your rocking boat over so that the stairs are facing up. Get a large, soft pillow or tumbling mat and set it next to the stairs.

Say *Jack And Jill* with the children as they climb up the *hill* and *fall-off* by jumping onto the pillow/mat. Clap for each other as everyone jumps. Play over and over again.

JACK AND JILL

Jack and Jill
    Went up the hill

To fetch
    A pail of water.

Jack fell down
    And broke his crown,

And Jill
    Came tumbling after.

JUMPED IN THE BOAT

Help Children:
- Become aware of numbers.
- Exercise their whole body.

IN THE BOAT

While the children are rocking in the rocking boat, sing *Jumped In The Boat*. As you are all singing the second verse *"fall out"* of the boat and climb back in. Sing over and over as the children climb in and out of the boat.

JUMPED IN THE BOAT

They jumped in the boat
  (Sit up straight.)
And the boat tipped over.
  (Bend to the side.)

They jumped in the boat
And the boat tipped over.

They jumped in the boat
And the boat tipped over.

Ten little boys and girls.
  (Clap.)

LITTLE CLOWNS

Help Children
- **Count.**
- **Anticipate and wait.**
- **Stand in one position.**

TUMBLE AND FALL
Pretend that you are clowns. Stand up tall and rigid as you say *Little Clowns*. At the end everyone fall down and roll around the floor. Clap, stand-up, and say the fingerplay again.

USE YOUR GLOVE
Duplicate 4 of the 5 clowns, cut them out, add a piece of Velcro® and attach them to your glove. Begin the rhyme with the four clowns standing tall.

See page 132 for full-size patterns.

LITTLE CLOWNS

Four little clowns stand up tall
1, 2, 3, 4.
> (*Hold up four fingers as you count.*)

Four little clowns tumble and fall.
4, 3, 2, 1, 0.
> (*Tuck fingers into your fist.*)

RING AROUND THE ROSIE

- Cooperate.
- Coordinate their bodies.
- Follow directions.

CIRCLE FUN

Stand in a circle, hold hands, and begin to walk while singing *Ring Around The Rosie.* When you sing, *"We all fall down"* everyone falls down to the floor. Laugh and clap for each other. Stand and play again.

VARIATION: Hold onto a parachute/bedsheet as you walk around in the circle singing the song. When you fall down cover up your legs with the chute/sheet.

RING AROUND THE ROSIE

Ring around the rosie
Pocketful of posie.

Ashes, ashes.
We all fall down.

Cows are in the meadow
   (Sing slowly.)
Lying down and sleeping.
   (Snore.)

Thunder, lightning
   (Pound floor.)
We all stand up.
   (Stand up.)

THE WIND

Help Children:
- **Understand opposites.**
- **Move in different directions.**
- **Manipulate a parachute.**

PARACHUTE FUN

Use a parachute or bedsheet.

Stand around the parachute holding on with both hands. Slowly wave it up and down with the children. Stop waving it and start walking around in a circle holding onto it with one or two hands.

After *warming-up* slowly say *The Wind* fingerplay with the children. As you very slowly say each line move your body and parachute in the designated direction:

- Stretch up high.
- Bend down low.
- Walk forwards.
- Walk backwards.
- Walk around in a circle.

THE WIND

Here we go up, up, up.
(High on tiptoes, arms up.)
Here we go down, down, down.
(Squat down.)

Here we go forward.
(Bend forward.)
Here we go backward.
(Bend backwards.)

Here we go round
(Twirl.)
And round.

THIS LITTLE CLOWN

Help Children:
- **Control their finger muscles.**
- **Count.**

THIS LITTLE CLOWN
Take off your shoes and/or socks. (A good time to do this activity is when your children naturally have their shoes/socks off, such as at naptime.) As you are all saying the fingerplay, touch your toes. Say it again touching the toes on the same or other foot.

USE YOUR GLOVE
Duplicate the five little clowns on page 37, cut them out, add a piece of Velcro® and attach them to your glove. Start with all of the clowns tucked into a fist. Raise them up as you say the fingerplay.

THIS LITTLE CLOWN

This little clown is happy and fat.
(Hold up 1 finger.)
This little clown does tricks with a cat.
(2 fingers.)
This little clown is tall and strong.
(3 fingers.)
This little clown sings a funny song.
(4 fingers.)
This little clown is wee and small.
(5 fingers.)
But he can do anything at all.
(Clap for the clowns.)

(Let the clowns fall down one at a time and form a fist again. Count "5, 4, 3, 2, 1" as they fall. Play again.)

WALKING, WALKING

Help Children:
- Move in different ways.
- Cooperate.
- Socialize.

WALK, HOP AND RUN
Add movements to the song and sing as you go.

WALK, HOP AND RUN

*Walking, walking,
Walking, walking.*

*Hop, hop, hop,
Hop, hop, hop.*

*Running, running, running,
Running, running, running.*

*Now we stop.
Now we flop.*

CHANGE THE TEMPO
Sing *Walking, Walking* over and over again. Each time sing it at a different tempo ranging from very slow to very fast. Move to the tempo you're singing.

WALKING, WALKING
(tune: Are You Sleeping?)

Walking, walking,
  (Walk in a circle.)
Walking, walking.

Walk, walk, walk,
Walk, walk, walk.

Walking, walking, walking,
Walking, walking, walking.

Now we stop!
  (Freeze.)
Now we flop!
  (Fall down.)

Planes Trains & More

HUNK OF TIN

HUNK OF TIN

I'm a little hunk of tin.
Nobody knows where I have been
I've got four tires
And a steering wheel.

I'm a car, car, car
Honk, honk.
(Touch nose twice.)
Rattle, rattle, rattle.
(Shake whole body.)
Stop! Stop!
*(Hand out in front;
other hand out in front.)*
Beep, beep.
(Pull ear lobe twice.)

Help Children:
- Become aware of numbers.
- Say words slowly.
- Talk about cars and where they go.

IN THE CAR
Slowly say *Hunk Of Tin* with the children. Give yourselves plenty time to do each movement. After the rhyme say to the children, *"When I ride in a car, I go to the store. Where do you go?"* Let the children tell you. Say *Hunk Of Tin* again.

DRIVE THE CAR
Use several boxes as pretend cars in the block area. Encourage the children to *"drive"* all around.

LET'S BE FIREFIGHTERS

Help Children:
- **Learn about firefighters.**
- **Sequence events.**
- **Learn fire safety.**

HURRY, HURRY

Pass out rhythm sticks or wrist bells. Sing as you tap your sticks or shake your bells. Clap when you get back to the station.

MEET THE FIREFIGHTERS

Set a date with a firefighter to visit your children. Ask if he could drive over in a fire truck and let the children tour it. Maybe he could bring extra firefighting clothes for the children to touch and explore. Sing *Let's Be Firefighters* for your guest.

FIRE DRILLS

Practice fire drills with the children. After you come in, sing *Let's Be Firefighters*.

LET'S BE FIREFIGHTERS
(tune: 1 Little, 2 Little, 3 Little Children)

Hurry, hurry drive the fire truck.
  (Drive.)
Hurry, hurry drive the fire truck.
Hurry, hurry drive the fire truck.
On a Sunday morning.

Hurry, hurry turn the corner...
  (Tip to one side.)

Hurry, hurry find the fire...
  (Look around.)

Hurry, hurry climb the ladder...
  (Hand over hand.)

Hurry, hurry spray the water...
  (Hold fire hose.)

Hurry, hurry back to the station...
  (Drive.)

PEANUT BUTTER

PEANUT BUTTER BALLS

<u>You'll Need</u>

1 cup natural peanut
   butter
3/4 cup honey
2 cups powdered milk
Large resealable bag

<u>To Make:</u> Wash your hands. Put the honey and the peanut butter in the resealable bag. Close it and mix the ingredients by pushing on the bag. Open the bag and pour the powdered milk into it. Close and mix the ingredients again. Open the bag and give each child a small spoonful of the mixture to roll into a ball or other shape. Eat them right away or put them on a plate. Serve with a drink.

PEANUT BUTTER

A peanut sat on the railroad track

His heart was all-a-flutter
   (Pound hand on heart.)

Along came a train -- the 5:15.
   (Rotate arms forward and back.)

Toot, toot -- Peanut Butter.
   (Loud train sounds.)

ROW YOUR BOAT

Help Children:
- **Play with a partner.**
- **Learn to rock.**
- **Develop coordination**

BACK AND FORTH
Pair up and sit on the floor facing each other. Hold hands and begin rocking back and forth. As you rock, sing *Row, Row, Row Your Boat.*

MORE SINGING AND ROCKING
While the children are rocking in the rocking boat and/or an adult (child) is rocking in a chair, have everybody who is nearby sing *Row, Row, Row Your Boat.*

Encourage the children to sing *Row, Row, Row Your Boat* to their dolls while rocking them in cradles, rocking chairs, and their arms .

ROW, ROW, ROW YOUR BOAT

Row, row, row your boat

Gently down the stream

Merrily, merrily, merrily, merrily

Life is but a dream.

RUB-A-DUB

Help Children:
- **Climb in and out of a container.**
- **Socialize.**

IN AND OUT
Use the rocking boat, wash tubs, or large boxes. Have hats for the children to wear. Put on the hats, climb into the tub and say the rhyme. As you name the *butcher*, the *baker*, and the *candlestick maker* fall out of the tub. Climb back in and play again and again and again.

BY MYSELF
Leave several hats in the *tub*. Put the *tub* on a rug. Let the children play and sing as they choose.

RUB-A-DUB

Rub-a-dub-dub

Three men/women in a tub.

The butcher.

The baker.

The candlestick maker.

THE TRAIN

Help Children:
- Learn opposites.
- Learn train safety.
- Become familiar with trains.

FINGER TRAIN

Pretend that the fingers on one hand are the train cars and your opposite arm is the track. As everyone says the fingerplay, run your fingers up and down your arms.

FIELD TRIP

Arrange with the ticket agent at your local train depot for the children to take a train ride from the local station to the next stop. Get off, take a walk and/or have a picnic at that stop, board the train and return to your station. (Remember to have enough adult supervision.)

THE TRAIN

Choo, choo, choo
(Say loudly.)

The train comes down the track.
(Rotate arms forward.)

Choo, choo, choo
(Say loudly.)

And runs right back.
(Rotate arms backwards.)

THE TRAIN CHUGGED

Help Children:
- **Practice sitting on a train.**
- **Learn train safety.**

ALL ABOARD

Before singing *The Train Went Over The Mountain,* have the children help you make a train with the chairs. Pretend that you are a conductor and take *"tickets"* from those who want to climb aboard. After everyone is on, sit in the engineer's seat, start the train, and sing as you chug along the tracks.

THE TRAIN CHUGGED OVER THE MOUNTAIN
(tune: The Bear Went Over the Mountain)

The train chugged over the mountain.
   (Rotate arms forward.)
The train chugged over the mountain.
The train chugged over the mountain.
To see what it could see.
   (Hand above eyes.)

To see what it could see.
   (Look around.)
To see what it could see.
The train chugged over the mountain.
   (Rotate arms forward.)
To see what it could see.

TRAIN FUN
Put train cars in the block area.

50

WHEELS ON THE BUS

Help Children:
- **Learn about different parts of a bus.**
- **Practice sitting on a bus.**
- **Name people who ride on a bus.**

GET ON THE BUS:
Before singing the *Wheels On The Bus*, have the children help you make a bus using the chairs. Sit in the driver's seat. Have those who want to take a bus ride, give you a *ticket* and choose a seat. When everyone's aboard, start the bus and begin singing.

WHEELS ON THE BUS

The wheels on the bus go round and round.
  (Roll arms.)
Round and round, round and round.
The wheels on the bus go round and round
All through the town.

The door on the bus goes open and shut....

The horn on the bus goes beep-beep-beep....

The lights on the bus turn on and off....

The windows on the bus go up and down....

The driver on the bus says, "Move on back."....

The babies on the bus go, "Waaa-waaa-waaa!"....

The mommies on the bus go, "Shhh-shhh-shhh!"....

Continue with the children's ideas.

WHEELS ON THE BUS

Help Children.
- Learn about different parts of a bus.
- Practice sitting on a bus.
- Name people who ride on a bus.

GET ON THE BUS:

Before singing the Wheels On The Bus, have the children help you make a bus using the chairs. Sit in the driver's seat. Have those who want to take a turn, give you a dollar and climb on the bus. When everyone is aboard, start the bus and begin singing.

WHEELS ON THE BUS

The wheels of the bus go round and round.

Round and round, round and round. The wheels of the bus go round and round.

The door on the bus goes open and shut...

The driver on the bus says move on back...

The baby on the bus goes wah-wah-wah...

The people on the bus go up and down...

The horn on the bus goes beep-beep-beep...

Self

HAPPY BIRTHDAY

HAPPY BIRTHDAY

Happy birthday to you.
(Point to friends.)

Happy birthday to you.
(Point to more friends.)

Happy birthday to everyone.
(Spread out arms.)

Happy birthday to you.
(Point to friends.)

Help Children:
- Socialize.
- Control rhythm sticks.
- Learn how to blow.

BLOW OUT THE CANDLES

Everyone sing *Happy Birthday*. At the end put your hands in the air with all of your fingers pointing straight up. Pretend that your fingers are birthday candles. Everyone blow them out.

RHYTHM STICK CANDLES

Give everyone rhythm sticks for birthday candles. While singing, have the "*candles*" sit on the cake by holding them straight up at your sides or out in front of you. After the song, hold the "*birthday candles*" in the air and blow them out. As they are blown out, lay them down on the floor.

IF YOU'RE HAPPY

Help Children:
- **Become aware of feelings.**
- **Socialize.**
- **Begin to take turns.**

PUPPET FUN
Get solid color paper plates and wide markers. Draw a feeling face on each paper plate. As you sing each verse have children (or you) hold up the appropriate plates and march around with them.

IF YOU'RE HAPPY AND YOU KNOW IT

If you're happy and you know it, clap your hands.
If you're happy and you know it, clap your hands.
If you're happy and you know it,
Then you're face will really show it.
If you're happy and you know it, clap your hands.

If you're sleepy and you know it, close your eyes......
   (Cover eyes.)

If you're sick and you know it cover your mouth......
   (Cough.)

If you're hungry and you know it rub your tummy......
   (Rub stomach.)

If you're sad and you know it rub your eyes......
   (Say "Boo-hoo")

LITTLE MISS MUFFET

LITTLE MISS MUFFET

Little Miss Muffet
Sat on her tuffet
Eating her curds and whey.
(Eat with hands.)

Along came a spider
And sat down beside her
And frightened
    Miss Muffet away.
(Shake whole body.)

Help Children:
- **Become familiar with position words.**

ALONG CAME A SPIDER
Get a small plastic spider and a two foot piece of yarn. Tie the spider to one end of the yarn. Show the spider to the children.

Hide the spider in the palm of your hand. Let a child be Miss Muffet and sit in a chair. Say the rhyme, using the child's name rather than Miss Muffet. At the appropriate time bring out the spider and let it sit *behind, in front of, next to, on top of,* or *under* the child. Everyone call out where the spider is, and the child runs back to the group. Play again and again.

HINT: If you don't have a plastic spider, paint a toilet paper roll black. When it's dry cut one end into 8 one inch slits.

ME

Help Children:
- **Balance.**
- **Learn opposites.**
- **Feel proud.**
- **Anticipate.**

TALL OR SMALL

Have all of the children sit in a group. Name a child. That child either crouches down as small as she can or stands on her tiptoes. The rest of the children call out -- *"Tall"* or *"Small"*

PEEK-A-BOO

Find several large, simple pictures of children crouching down and standing tall. (Catalogues are great resources.) Back each one with felt. Have the children cover their eyes. Put one picture on the felt board. Say, *"Peek-a-boo."* The children peek through their fingers and shout out *"tall"* or *"small"* depending on the picture. Cover up and play over and over again with the same and different pictures.

ME

I can stand
Up very tall.
  (Stand on tiptoes.)
Then make myself
Very, very small.
  (Crouch down.)

I can be quiet
As quiet can be.
  (Finger touching lips.)
But here I am
Just being ME!
  (Jump and shout "ME")

MITTEN WEATHER

MITTEN WEATHER

Thumbs in the thumb place,
(Stick out thumb.)

Fingers all together.
(Squeeze fingers together.)

This is the song we sing

In mitten weather.

Help Children:
- Put on and take off their mittens.
- Learn about cold weather.

MITTEN TIME
Children need opportunities to practice putting on and taking off their mittens. Bring out a box of mittens and pass them out or have the children use their own.

Let the children put on their mittens. As they do, slowly repeat the first two lines of *Mitten Weather*. Clap for each child after she's gotten her mittens on. After everyone has mittens on say the entire fingerplay together.

VARIATIONS:
- Keep mittens handy. Practice putting them on and taking them off with individual children.
- Put mittens in the housekeeping area for children to use on their own.
- Say the rhyme as you're dressing to go outside on cold days.

NAME GAME

Help Children:
- **Know names.**
- **Play with words.**
- **Be silly.**

PASS THE TOY

Have one of the children's favorite stuffed toys nearby. Start the rhyme by holding the toy and using your name. After you and the toy have bowed and everyone has clapped for you, pass the toy to someone else. Say the rhyme using the child's name. Continue passing the toy and playing the *Name Game*.

NAME CARDS

On large strips of white posterboard write each child's name. Hold up one name card. Read the name. Say the rhyme using that child's name. Clap! Continue.

HINT: If a child isn't playing the game, use his name anyhow. He will hear it from where he is.

NAME GAME

Liz Liz Bo Biz
  (Clap to beat.)
Banana Fana Fo Fiz
Me My Mo Miz
Liz.
  (Child bows. Everyone claps.)

Substitute children's names and change last word in each line to rhyme.

_____ _____ Bo B ____
Banana Fana Fo F ____
Me My Mo M ____

_____
  (Yeh! Clap!)

PEANUT BUTTER AND JELLY

Help Children:
- **Learn to hum.**
- **Make a simple snack.**
- **Practice healthy habits.**

CRACKER SANDWICHES
<u>You'll Need</u>:
Crackers
Peanut butter
Natural jelly
Popsicle sticks

<u>To Make</u>: Wash your hands. Use popsicle sticks to spread peanut butter and jelly on some of the crackers. Top each one with a plain cracker. Enjoy your sandwiches with a drink.

PEANUT BUTTER AND JELLY

Peanut, peanut butter -- and jelly
   (Shout peanut; whisper jelly.)
Peanut, peanut butter -- and jelly
Peanut, peanut butter -- and jelly.

First you take a peanut and you smush it, smush it.
   (Rub hands together.)
First you take a peanut and you smush it, smush it.

Peanut, peanut butter -- and jelly...... *(Hum.)*

Then you take a knife and you spread it, spread it.
   (Spread one palm with opposite fingers.)
Then you take a knife and you spread it, spread it.

Peanut, peanut butter -- and jelly......*(Hum)*

Then you take bread and you fold it, fold it. *(Close hand.)*
Then you take bread and you fold it, fold it.

Peanut, peanut butter -- and jelly......*(Hum.)*

Then you take the sandwich and you bite it, bite it. *(Chew.)*
Then you take the sandwich and you bite it, bite it.

Peanut, peanut butter -- and jelly......*(Hum.)*

Help Children:

- Learn about body space.
- Socialize.
- Feel 'tricky.'

PEEK-A-BOO ALL DAY THROUGH

Play different peek-a-boo games throughout the day:

- Hide checkers or small blocks in the sand table.
- Hang a light-weight blanket over your full-length mirror. Let the children play *peek-a-boo* with themselves as they lift the blanket and look in the mirror.
- Hold a scarf over your face. Go up to a child and say the *Peek-a-Boo* rhyme.
- Watch for children who are playing in small hideouts such as under tables, behind chairs, or next to shelves. Quietly walk over and say, *"Peek-a-boo, I see you."*
- Have a *mystery purse* and put different *things* in it.

PEEK-A-BOO

Peek-a-boo
(Hands over face.)

I see you!
(Spread fingers and peek at others.)

USE YOUR EYES

Help Children:
- **Become aware of clothes.**
- **Notice detail.**

FELT BOARD FUN

Using different colored pieces of felt, cut clothes which the children wear. As you name each piece of clothing in the rhyme, put the matching felt piece on the board.

USE YOUR EYES

Use your eyes,
 (Point to your eyes.)
Use your eyes.
You can look
And see.

If you're wearing
Socks.
 *(Stop and let childen
 look.)*
Point them out
 (Children touch socks.)
To me.

(See page 133 for full-sized patterns.)

WATCH WHAT I DO

Help Children:
- **Imitate movements.**
- **Exercise small muscles.**
- **Exercise large muscles.**

SMALL MOVEMENTS
Sit down with the children. Say the rhyme. Do a small muscle movement:

- Nod your head.
- Wiggle a finger.
- Wave a hand.
- Bend your leg.
- Twist your foot.

Let the children copy you. Repeat.

GIANT MOVEMENTS
Stand up with the children. Say the rhyme. Do a large muscle movement:

- March.
- Swing your legs.
- Bow down and up.
- Swing your arms.
- Turn your body around.
- Skate around the floor.

WATCH WHAT I DO

Watch what I do.
Watch what I do.
   (Do a movement.)

Now you do it.
Now you do it.
   (Everyone do movement.)

Repeat with different movements for children to follow.

WE GET DRESSED

DRESS THE DOLL

Cut out a simple felt child and his/her clothes. Put the child and all of the clothes on the felt board. Point to each piece of clothing and name it with the children.

Begin singing *We Get Dressed*. As you sing each verse, dress the felt child. (Add verses and clothes which are appropriate for your children.)

WE GET DRESSED
(tune: Here We Go Round the Mulberry Bush)

This is the way that we get dressed
We get dressed, we get dressed.
This is the way that we get dressed
Everyday of the year.

This is the way we put on our shirts...

This is the way we put on our pants...

This is the way we put on our socks...

This is the way we put on our shoes...

Last verse: Repeat first verse.

WHERᴇ, OH WHERᴇ IS

Help Children:
- Learn their names.
- Transition.

GATHERING THE CHILDREN
Walk around the room singing *Where Oh Where Is*. As you name a child she finishes what she is doing and comes with you. After you've gathered several children, begin moving to the new activity such as lunch, group time, or a neighborhood walk. Continue singing and naming other children, encouraging them to join you.

COVER-UP
Cover up your faces with your hands. Sing *Where, Oh Where Is*. As you name a child everyone uncovers their faces. The child you named, comes over to you and hugs you while everyone else claps. Everyone cover up and play again.

PEEK-A-BOO
Sing the song with individual children as they:

- Wake up from naps.
- Play in *hide-outs*.

WHERE, OH WHERE IS
(tune: Here We Go Round the Mulberry Bush)

Where, oh where is (child's name)?
   (Hands above eyes looking for the child.)

Is (child's name), is (child's name)?

Where, oh where is (child's name)?

Peek-a-boo

I see you!

Our Bodies

ALL OF ME

ON THE DOLL
Have a large doll. As you slowly say the rhyme, hold up the doll and touch each of her body parts as the children touch theirs. Clap *hooray* at the end.

EXTENSION: Put the doll in the housekeeping area. As you are playing with the children, talk about the different body parts again. Have them point to and name the doll's parts. Maybe they can also find their own again.

ALL OF ME

See my eyes. *(Touch eyes.)*
See my nose. *(Touch nose.)*
See my chin. *(Touch chin.)*
See my toes. *(Touch toes.)*

See my waist. *(Touch waist.)*
See my knees. *(Touch knees.)*
See my arms. *(Touch arm.)*
Now you've seen all of me.
    (Raise arms.)

CLAP HANDS

Help Children:
- **Wait.**
- **Count.**
- **Exercise their hands.**

WAIT
Say this fingerplay with an individual child or a group of children anytime during the day while you are waiting for something or someone, such as:

- Lunch to start.
- The group to gather.
- Everyone to get ready.

FOLLOW ME
As you say the first line of each verse, do the action in a little different position, such as clap your hands over your head, shake your hands near the floor, etc. As you say the second line of each verse encourage the children to do that action with you.

CLAP HANDS

Clap your hands 1, 2, 3
(Clap.)
Clap your hands just like me.
(Clap again.)

Roll your hands 1, 2, 3...
(Roll.)

Tap your hands 1, 2, 3...
(Tap.)

Shake your hands 1, 2, 3...
(Shake.)

Bend your hands 1, 2, 3...
(Bend.)

CLAP YOUR HANDS

Help Children:
- **Exercise their whole body.**
- **Identify body parts.**

CLAP NOW OR THEN

Sing the first verse of the song over and over. Each time you sing, clap your hands in a different place, such as over your heads, out in front of you, behind your backs, at your knees, etc.

CLAP LOUDLY

Sing the first verse of *Clap Your Hands* over and over again. The first time you sing, clap as loudly as possible. Each subsequent time clap a little more softly until you are making no noise. Then sing one more time making as much noise as possible. Clap for each other!

CLAP YOUR HANDS
(tune: Jingle Bells)

Clap your hands
   (Clap hands to the beat.)
Clap your hands
Clap them just like me

Oh what fun
It is to clap
And sing so happily.

Touch your toes...
Stretch your arms...
Walk your legs...
Row your boat...
Throw your ball...

EARLY IN THE MORNING

Help Children:
- **Learn body parts.**
- **Move body parts.**
- **Follow directions.**

SIMON SAYS
Before singing *Early In The Morning,* play *Simon Says* using all of the movements in the song.

Simon says,

- *"Clap your hands."*
- *"Stomp your feet."*
- *"Shake your legs."*
- *"Twist your heads."*
- *"Wiggle your toes."*
- *"Bend your fingers."*
- *"Wiggle your noses."*
- *"Blink your eyes."*
- *"Yawn your mouth."*
- *"Swing your arms."*

EARLY IN THE MORNING

This is the way we clap our hands, *(Clap.)*
Clap our hands, clap our hands.
This is the way we clap our hands,
So early in the morning.

Stomp our feet. *(March.)*
Shake our legs. *(Shake.)*
Nod our heads. *(Nod.)*
Wiggle our toes. *(Wiggle.)*
Bend our fingers. *(Bend.)*
Wiggle our noses. *(Wiggle.)*
Blink our eyes. *(Blink.)*
Yawn our mouth. *(Yawn.)*
Swing our arms. *(Swing.)*

FEE, FIE, FOE, FUM

Help Children:
- Play with their voices.
- March in place.
- Identify fingers and thumbs.
- Balance.

MARCH

Pretend that you are all *giants* with deep, slow voices. Say the rhyme together.

After saying it with your *giant voices* several times, begin to march in place as you say it. Get your legs up high. Remember, you're *giants*.

FEE, FIE, FOE, FUM

Fee, fie, foe, fum!
See my fingers.
   (Hold up fingers.)
See my thumbs.
   (Hold up thumbs.)

Fee, fie, foe, fum!
Fingers gone.
   (Hide fingers.)
So are thumbs.
   (Hide thumbs.)

HEAD, SHOULDERS

Help Children:
- **Identify body parts.**
- **Follow directions.**

HEAD AND SHOULDERS
Pass the rhythm sticks to the children. Using a very slow, whisper voice say the first verse of the fingerplay together. As you say each body part, let the children touch it with their sticks.

Clap the sticks together and sing the rhyme again.

SIMON SAYS
Slowly sing *Head, Shoulders, Knees, And Toes* with the children. Now play *Simon Says*.

Simon should direct the children to point to different body parts. Begin with the parts mentioned in the fingerplay and then expand to others.

HEAD, SHOULDERS, KNEES, AND TOES

Head, shoulders,
    (Touch each body part.)
Knees, and toes,
Knees and toes,
Knees and toes.

Head, shoulders,
Knees, and toes,
Eyes, ears,
Mouth and nose.

HOKEY-POKEY

HOKEY-POKEY

You put your one arm in. *(Arm in front.)*
You put your one arm out. *(Arm in back.)*
You put your one arm in. *(Arm in front.)*
And you shake it all about. *(Shake arm.)*

You do the hokey-pokey, *(Arms in air.)*
And you turn yourself around. *(Twirl.)*
That's what it's all about. *(Clap.)*

Continue with other body parts:
*   Other arm...*
*   One leg...other leg.*
*   One elbow...other elbow.*
*   Continue.*
*   End with whole self.*

Help Children:
- **Identify body parts.**
- **Learn opposites.**
- **Sing at different speeds.**
- **Control rhythm instruments.**

FASTER - SLOWER
Sing and play *Hokey Pokey* at different speeds. You could:

- Start out very slowly, get slightly faster with each verse, and be the fastest on the last verse when you put your whole body in.
- Sing and dance the entire song in slow or fast motion.
- Give your children the choice of whether they want to sing and play fast or slow.

RING THE BELLS
Give everyone wrist bells or clappers. Shake them each time you dance the *Hokey-Pokey*.

I'M HIDING

Help Children:
- Anticipate.
- Listen.
- Identify body parts.

LISTEN CAREFULLY
Say the rhyme with the children adding a third body part to the fourth line. When the children hear you name it, they should poke it out. Then everyone jump up and shout, *"Surprise!"*

For example:
I'm hiding, I'm hiding
And no-one knows where
For all you can see
Is my <u>*head*</u>*, toes, and*
    hair.
Surprise!

I'M HIDING

I'm hiding, I'm hiding
    (*Curl up and cover*
    head with hands.)
And no-one knows where,
For all you can see
Is my toes and my hair.
    (*Pause.*)

Surprise! (*Jump up.*)

OPEN THEM, SHUT THEM

Help Children:
- Learn opposites.
- Name body parts.

CREEP THEM
After the children can open and shut their hands, play *Creep Them*. To begin, name and touch different parts of your arms and faces. (fingers, wrists, elbows, chins, mouths, etc.) Now say *Open Them, Shut Them* with the children and add the verse below.

Creep them, creep them
(Walk fingers up arms.)
Up to your chin.
Open your mouth
(Open mouth.)
But do not let them in.
(Shake head 'no'.)

Repeat the first two verses.

OPEN THEM, SHUT THEM

Open them, shut them.
   (Open and close your fists.)
Open them, shut them.
Open them, shut them.
Give a little clap.
   (Clap.)

Open them, shut them.
   (Open and close your fists.)
Open them, shut them.
Open them, shut them.
Lay them in your lap.
   (Set hands in lap.)

PAT-A-CAKE

Help Children:
- **Learn their names.**
- **Develop self-esteem.**
- **Become aware of letters.**
- **Develop hand coordination**

FOR ME

Play with individual children. Say the first verse and do the actions to *Pat-A-Cake*.

Change the second verse to reflect the child's first initial and name, thus in the second line you would mark the cake with the letter of the child's name rather than the *"B"* and substitute the child's name for *Baby* in the last line. After saying the rhyme, hug each other. For example:

Roll it, pat it
And mark it with a C
Put it in the oven
For Cheryl and me.

PAT-A-CAKE

Pat-a-cake, pat-a-cake
  (Clap hands.)
Baker's man.
Bake me a cake
As fast as you can.

Roll it, pat it,
  (Roll hands, pat hands together.)
And mark it with a B.
Put it in the oven
  (Arms out in front.)
For Baby and me.
  (Hug self.)

UP, UP, UP

Help Children:
- Learn body parts.
- Know their names.
- Develop self-esteem.

TOUCH

Adapt this fingerplay to do with an individual child. Hold a child's hands and say the fingerplay and do the movements together. Change the words of the fingerplay each time to name the child you're playing with. For example:

Up, up, up,
(Child's name) *goes.*
Reach way up
And touch your nose.

Down, down, down,
(Child's name) *goes*
Reach way down
And touch your toes.

UP, UP, UP

Up, up, up, *(Lift arms up.)*
The children go.
Reach way up
And touch our nose. *(Touch nose.)*

Down, down, down, *(Bend down.)*
The children go.
Reach way down
And touch our toes.
   (Touch toes.)

   Continue up and down naming and touching other body parts.

WASH OUR BODIES

Help Children:
- **Identify body parts.**
- **Stay healthy.**

WASH OUR FACES
After your children are familiar with all of their major body parts, change the words of the song to help them learn specific body parts.

WASH OUR FACES
This is the way
We wash our faces,
Wash our faces,
Wash our faces.

This is the way
We wash our faces
Everyday
Of the week.

Chins......
Mouths......
Noses......
Cheeks......
Eyes......
Forehead......

Last verse: Repeat first verse.

WASH OUR BODIES
(tune: Here We Go Round the Mulberry Bush)

This is the way we wash our bodies
Wash our bodies, wash our bodies.
This is the way we wash our bodies,
Everyday of the week.

Our feet...... *(Wash feet.)*

Our legs...... *(Wash legs.)*

Our tummies...... *(Wash stomachs.)*

Arms...... *(Wash arms.)*

Chests...... *(Wash chests.)*

Faces...... *(Wash faces.)*

Hair...... *(Wash hair.)*

Last verse: Repeat first verse.

WATCH MY FEET

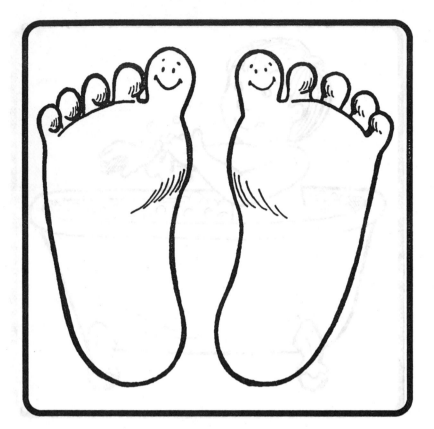

Help Children:
- **Move in different ways.**
- **Expand their vocabulary.**
- **Learn body parts.**

WATCH MY HANDS
Expand this rhyme to feature other body parts and movements. For example:

Watch my <u>hands</u>
(Hold up 2 hands.)
They're coming to play.
My two hands
Are (name movement)
today! (shaking, waving, clapping, opening, closing, etc.)

Watch my <u>head</u>
It's coming to play.
My one head
Is (name movement) *to-day!* (nodding, rolling around, jerking, etc.)

WATCH MY FEET

Watch my feet.
 (Put foot out.)

They're coming to play.

My two feet

Are *(name movement)* today!
 (Do movement.)

Dick Wilmes

WE WIGGLE

Help Children:
- **Identify body parts.**
- **Know their names.**

I WIGGLE
Repeat this fingerplay throughout the day with individual children. Say it at a comfortable pace for each child, so that she has plenty of time to wiggle each of her body parts. Change the words to name the child you're playing with. "(Child's name) *wiggles his fingers...*"

WIGGLE SOME MORE
Say the fingerplay. Add more verses by changing the first and third lines of the fingerplay to name other body parts. For example:

We wiggle our elbows.
We wiggle our toes.
We wiggle our legs.
We wiggle our nose.

Continue, naming and wiggling other body parts.

WE WIGGLE

We wiggle our fingers.
  (Move fingers.)

We wiggle our toes.
  (Move toes.)

We wiggle our shoulders.
  (Move shoulders.)

We wiggle our nose.
  (Move nose.)

WHERE ARE YOUR EYES?

Help Children:
- **Learn about their senses.**
- **Name body parts.**

FELT BOARD FUN
Find large magazine pictures of people, preferably young children, using each of their senses. Cut out each picture, glue it to a piece of construction paper, cover the front side with clear adhesive paper, and put felt on the backside.

Bring the feltboard and pictures. Put the first picture on the feltboard. Sing the first verse. Put the second picture on the feltboard and sing the second verse. Continue with all of the five senses.

WHERE ARE YOUR EYES?

Where are your eyes? Show me your eyes -
Your eyes can see.
Where are your eyes? Show me your eyes -
Shut them quietly.

Where is your nose? Show me your nose -
Your nose can smell.
Where is your nose? Show me your nose -
Wiggle it well.

Where is your mouth? Show me your mouth -
It can open wide.
Where is your mouth? Show me your mouth -
Lots of teeth inside.

WHERE IS THUMBKIN?

Help Children:
- **Coordinate their thumbs and fingers.**
- **Make fists.**
- **Socialize.**

THUMB TALK
Early in the day use a ball point pen to draw a simple *smiley face* on every child's thumb. While you're playing, use your *thumb puppets* to wave at and talk with each child.

SMILING THUMBKIN
Sing *Where Is Thumbkin* throughout the day, encouraging everyone to use their *smiley face* thumbs. (See *Thumb Talk*.)

WHERE IS THUMBKIN?

Where is thumbkin, where is thumbkin?
  (Fists behind back.)

Here I am, here I am!
  (One thumb, then other out front.)

How are you today sir?
  (Wiggle one thumb.)

Very well I thank you.
  (Wiggle other thumb.)

Run away, run away!
  (One fist, then other behind back.)

Help Children:
- Coordinate their thumbs and fingers.
- Make fists.
- Socialize

WHERE IS THUMBKIN?

Rest
&
Relax

ARE YOU SLEEPING?

Help Children:
- **Relax.**
- **Control bells.**
- **Anticipate.**

BELLS ARE RINGING
Everyone lie down on the floor and begin singing. After the first verse pause to wake up and stretch. Pass out the bells and shake them as you sing the second verse.

WAKE UP
As you walk around the cots to wake up the children, softly sing this song while you quietly shake the bells.

ARE YOU SLEEPING?

Are you sleeping?
 (Close eyes.)
Are you sleeping?
Brother John,
Brother John.

Morning bells are ringing,
 (Open eyes.)
Morning bells are ringing.
Ding, ding, dong.
 *(Gently shake hands as
 if ringing bells.)*
Ding, ding, dong.

CRISS-CROSS APPLESAUCE

Help Children:
- **Relax.**
- **Feel loved.**
- **Learn to blow.**

ON THE COT
As the children are lying down for naps or just beginning to wake up from them, quietly say *Criss-Cross Applesauce* while gently doing the actions.

TAKE-A-MINUTE
When you notice that a child is having a problem or seems frustrated, walk over to her, and ask her to take a deep breath. While she's taking her breath, slowly and gently say *Criss-Cross Applesauce* and do the actions.

ADULT'S TURN
Turn around and let a child or small group of children say the rhyme and do the actions up your back.

CRISS-CROSS APPLESAUCE

Criss-cross applesauce.
    (Draw X with finger on child's back.)

Spiders crawling up your spine.
    (Walk fingers up child's back.)

Cool breeze.
    (Gently blow on child's neck.)

Tight squeeze.
    (Hug child.)

Makes you get the sillies.
    (Gently tickle child.)

GO TO SLEEP

Help Children:
• Relax.

NAPTIME BACK RUBS
Have body lotion nearby your cots. Kneel down next to a child. Very gently begin to rub her back and quietly sing *Go To Sleep.*

Put a little lotion on your fingers and rub her arms and shoulders. Repeat for all of the children who have not fallen asleep.

GO TO SLEEP
(tune: Here We Go Round the Mulberry Bush)

This is the way we go to sleep
(Sing quietly.)

Go to sleep, go to sleep.

This is the way we go to sleep

Every afternoon.

Repeat until everyone is resting.

3 LITTLE CHILDREN

Help Children:
- **Become aware of numbers.**
- **Transition to other activities.**
- **Follow directions.**

EXTEND THE SONG

Use this song to help children move from one activity to another, such as from free choice to lunch, or nap, or outdoors.

Sing the first verse of the song to alert the children, and then add the additional verses while moving. Encourage the children to sing with you as they move.

For example

- *They swam to their cubbies and we said good-bye...*

- *They swam to the table and we sang 'til lunch...*

- *They swam to the door and we walked outside...*

1 LITTLE, 2 LITTLE, 3 LITTLE CHILDREN

1 little, 2 little, 3 little children,
   (Point at children while singing.)
4 little, 5 little, 6 little children,
7 little, 8 little, 9 little children,
10 little boys and girls.

They swam and they swam and they swam to their cots.
They swam and they swam and they swam to their cots.
They swam and they swam and they swam to their cots.
Ten little boys and girls.
   (Slowly and quietly sing.)

We hugged and we kissed and we put them into bed.
We hugged and we kissed and we put them into bed.
We hugged and we kissed and we put them into bed.
Ten little boys and girls.

QUIET

NAPTIME

Tiptoe around the children lying on their cots. If someone is having difficulty settling down, bend over and rub the child's shoulders. As you're doing so, whisper *Quiet*. As you get up gently say, *"Good night, (child's name). Sleep tight."*

QUIET

Now the wiggles

Are out of us
(Stand limp.)

And we're as quiet

As we can be.
(Finger over mouths.)

Shhhhh.
(Very quietly.)

ROCK-A-BYE BABY

Help Children:
- Nurture their "babies."
- Rock.

ROCK AND SING
Put dolls in all areas of the classroom. Rock the dolls and sing to them:

- In the cradle in housekeeping.
- In the rocking chair near the books.
- In the rocking boat on a rug.
- In your arms anyplace in the room.

ROCK-A-BYE BABY

Rock-a-bye baby
  (Rock a pretend baby.)
In the treetop.
When the wind blows
The cradle will rock.

When the bough breaks
The cradle will fall.
  (Gently drop to floor.)
Down will come baby
Cradle and all.

SOFT KITTY

Help Children:
• **Play with their voices.**

MEOW SOFT KITTY

Ask the children if any of them have or know cats. Let them *meow* like their pets.

After everyone has *meowed* have them follow your directions using different cat voices:

"Meow very loudly."

"Meow like a giant cat."

"Meow in a squeaky voice."

"Meow like a scared cat."

"Meow like a happy cat."

"Meow like a sad cat."

"Meow like an angry cat."

"Meow in a whisper voice."

SOFT KITTY

Soft kitty, warm kitty.
   (Make a fist.)

Little ball of fur.
   (Pet your kitty.)

Lazy kitty, pretty kitty.

"Purr, purr, purr."

SHHHHH !

Help Children:
- **Relax.**
- **Use a whisper voice.**

NAPTIME

As you are helping the children settle down for their naps, whisper *SHHHHH!* with them. Gently rub their arms to help them rest, relax, and fall asleep. Tiptoe away.

SHHHHH!

Shhhhh --- be very quiet.
(Finger over mouth.)
Shhhhh --- be very still.
(Finger over mouth.)

Rest your busy, busy arms.
(Hang them at your sides.)
Close your sleepy, sleepy eyes.
(Close eyes.)

Shhhhh --- be very still.
(Lie down.)
Good night.
(Whisper.)

TEDDY BEAR

Help Children:
- Exercise their whole body.
- Follow directions from a puppet.
- Follow a series of directions.

EXERCISE WITH TEDDY
Get a stuffed or puppet teddy bear. (You could enlarge and duplicate the Teddy Bear pattern to make a simple stick puppet.) Introduce Teddy to the children. Let him teach the children the words and actions to the *Teddy Bear* rhyme. Say and do it together.

TEDDY BEAR PARADES
Let Teddy Bear lead the children as they:

- March around the room.
- Play *Follow The Leader*.
- Walk around the neighborhood.

TEDDY BEAR

Teddy bear, teddy bear
   turn around.
Teddy bear, teddy bear
   touch the ground.

Teddy bear, teddy bear
   walk upstairs.
Teddy bear, teddy bear
   brush your hairs.

Teddy bear, teddy bear
   turn out the light.
Teddy bear, teddy bear
   say, "Good night!"

TEN LITTLE FINGERS

Help Children:
- **Coordinate their hand/finger muscles.**
- **Learn opposites.**

HIDE A TOY

Collect lots of small toys (block, matchbox car, finger puppet, crayon, doll, ball, etc.) at least one for each child. Put them in a *mystery bag.* Say *Ten Little Fingers.* At the end walk around to each child, secretly pull out a toy from your *mystery bag* and put it in her folded hands. Everyone name the toy she got and put it back into the *bag.* Say the rhyme again and hide new toys.

WARM UP

Before saying *Ten Little Fingers* do some warm-up exercises such as:

- *Shake your hands.*
- *Spread your fingers.*
- *Open/shut your hands.*
- *Wiggle your fingers.*
- *Make tight fists - Relax.*

TEN LITTLE FINGERS

I have ten little fingers.
They all belong to me.

I can make them do things.
Would you like to see?

I can close them up tight.
I can open them up wide.

I can hold them up high.
I can hold them down low.

I can wave them to and fro.
And I can fold them just so.

TWO LITTLE FEET

TWO LITTLE FEET

Two little feet go tap, tap, tap.
   (March.)
Two little hands go clap, clap, clap.
   (Clap.)

Two little feet go jump, jump, jump.
   (Jump.)
Two little hands go thump, thump, thump.
   (Tap thighs.)

One little body turns round and round.
   (Turn around.)
And sits quietly down.
   (Sit down.)

Help Children:
- **Learn new movements.**
- **Relax**
- **Listen carefully.**

ROUND AND ROUND
Form a circle and go *round and round* using different actions. Say, *"Skate round and round."* Everyone skate in a circle and then say, *"Stop."* Continue with other actions:

* *Jump*
* *Fly*
* *Tiptoe*
* *March*
* *Walk*

LISTEN CAREFULLY
Say *Two Little Hands* with the children. Change the last stanza so that the children use a different movement as they turn round and round. Be sure to say the new action word slowly and distinctly. In the beginning you might even say, *"One little body (now listen carefully) tiptoes round and round..."*

TWINKLE, TWINKLE

Help Children:
- **Strengthen hand muscles.**
- **Relax.**

SHHHH! IT'S NAPTIME
While the children are getting ready for naptime, very quietly sing *Twinkle, Twinkle Little Star*. Repeat it several times, each time singing more slowly and softly.

If several children have not calmed down, tiptoe over to their cots, kneel down and sing quietly to them. As you're singing, rub their backs and shoulders.

TWINKLE, TWINKLE LITTLE STAR

Twinkle, twinkle little star,
(Open and close your hands.)
How I wonder what you are.

Up above the world so high,
(Twinkle hands high.)
Like a diamond in the sky.

Twinkle, twinkle little star,
How I wonder what you are.

Help Children:
- Strengthen hand muscles.
- Relax.

SHHHHH! IT'S NAPTIME

While the children are getting ready for naptime, very quietly sing Twinkle, Twinkle Little Star. Repeat it several times, each time singing more slowly and softly.

If several children have lain down, tiptoe one to their cots, kneel down and sing quietly to each one. As you're singing, rub their backs and shoulders.

TWINKLE, TWINKLE
LITTLE STAR

Twinkle, twinkle, little star,
How I wonder what you are.

Up above the world so high,
Like a diamond in the sky.

Twinkle, twinkle, little star,
How I wonder what you are.

Animals

Farm

Zoo

Forest

BAA, BAA BLACK SHEEP

Help Children:
- Be aware of numbers.
- Develop fine motor skills.
- Cooperate.

STUFF THE BAG

Get a small garbage bag and old newspaper. Tear the newspaper into small pieces.

As everyone is singing, wad up the pieces of paper and stuff them into the bag. Sing again and again filling the bag fuller each time. When it is full, tie it closed and save it. Fill two more bags as you did the first one and save them. After you've filled all three bags, use them as you sing. Give them to the children as you sing, *"One for my master,"* etc. When you sing again, the children can give the bags to others. Continue.

BAA, BAA BLACK SHEEP

Baa, baa black sheep,
    have you any wool?
Yes sir, yes sir,
    (Shake head yes.)
Three bags full.
    (Hold up 3 fingers.)

One for my master.
    (Hold up 1 finger.)
One for my dame.
    (Hold up 1 finger.)
One for the little boy
    who cries in the lane.
    (Hold up 1 finger. Wipe eyes.)

FIVE LITTLE DUCKS

Help Children:
- **Learn to squat and waddle.**
- **Practice balance.**
- **Become aware of numbers.**

WADDLE TO THE RIVER
Pretend that a clothesline is the river. Lay it in an open area of the room.

Begin singing *Five Little Ducks*. While you are singing, squat down and waddle to the river, around it, and back again. Clap. Move the river, and sing and waddle again.

(See page 138 for full-sized patterns.)

FIVE LITTLE DUCKS

Five little ducks that I once knew.
(Wave 5 fingers in the air.)
Fat ones, skinny ones, tall ones too.
But the one little duck
With the feather on her back
(Wave hands behind back.)
She led the others with a
"Quack, quack, quack --- Quack, quack, quack."
(Clap hands.)

Down to the river they would go
(Squat and waddle around.)
Wibble-wobble, wibble-wobble to and fro
But the one little duck
With the feather on her back
(Wave hands behind back.)
She led the others with a
"Quack, quack, quack --- Quack, quack, quack."
(Clap hands.)

Up from the river they would come.
(Continue to waddle.)
Wibble-wobble, wibble-wobble, to and fro.
But the one little duck
With the feather on her back
(Wave hands behind back.)
She lead the others with a
"Quack, quack, quack --- Quack, quack, quack."
(Clap hands.)

FIVE LITTLE DUCKS PLAY

Help Children:
- **Play with their voices.**
- **Become aware of numbers.**
- **Enjoy repetition.**

USE YOUR GLOVE
Duplicate, cut out, and put a piece of Velcro® on the 5 small ducks and then attach them to your Velcro® glove. As you and the children say the rhyme, hold up the appropriate number of ducks. Open and shut your hands like a mama duck's bill, as you all call out, *"Quack, quack, quack!"*

FIVE LITTLE DUCKS WENT OUT TO PLAY

Five little ducks went out to play,
  (Raise 5 fingers.)
Over the hill and far away.
  (Wave good-bye to the duck.)
Mama Duck called, "Quack, quack, quack."
  (Shout.)
One little duck came swimming back.
  (Put down 1 finger.)

Four little ducks went out to play......
Three little ducks went out to play......
Two little ducks went out to play......

One little duck went out to play,
Over the hill and far away.
Mama duck yelled, "Quack, quack, quack!!"
Five little ducks came swimming back.

(See page 138 for full-sized patterns.)

GITTY-UP

Help Children:
- Learn rhythm.
- Control rhythm sticks.

GITTY-UP

Give everyone rhythm sticks. Pretend that you are horses galloping down the road by tapping the floor as you sing together.

After you are familiar with the song and the game, change the tempo. Sing the song and tap the floor very slowly, as if you are horses just walking down the road. Another time sing and tap the floor very quickly, as if you are horses racing down the road. Remember to clap after each horse ride.

GITTY-UP

Gitty-up, gitty-up, gitty-up
Up -- up!

Gitty-up, gitty-up, gitty-up,
Up -- up!

Gitty-up, gitty-up, gitty-up,
Up -- up!

Whooooa -------- Horsey
*(Raise arms high
in the air.)*

KITTEN CRAWLS

Help Children:
- **Move like animals.**
- **Sound like animals.**

FOLLOW THE LEADER
Sit with the children and sing the first verse of *Kitten Crawls*. Then pretend that you are kittens and crawl around the room making kitten sounds. After awhile stop being kittens, sit back down, and sing about another animal such as a bird. Pretend you are birds and fly around the room making bird sounds. Continue, pretending to be lots of other animals.

KITTEN CRAWLS
(tune: Here We Go Round the Mulberry Bush)

This is the way the kitten crawls,
  (Crawl in place.)
Kitten crawls, kitten crawls,
This is the way the kitten crawls,
On a sunny morning.

    Horse...gallops

    Puppy...runs

    Bird...flies

    Rabbit...hops

OLD MAC DONALD

Help Children:
- Distinguish animals.
- Add sound variations to their vocabulary.

FARM ANIMALS

Duplicate the farm animals, cut them out, and back each one with a piece of Velcro®. Have the animals and your Velcro® glove nearby.

Put on your glove. Put the cow on one finger and begin singing *Old Mac Donald*. Have the children name another animal. Put that one on a second finger and continue singing. Keep singing and adding animals.

(See page 134 for full-sized patterns.)

OLD MAC DONALD

Old Mac Donald had a farm --
    E-I-E-I-O.

And on his farm he had a cow --
    E-I-E-I-O.

With a "moo-moo" here,
    and a "moo-moo" there,

Here a "moo", there a "moo"

Everywhere a "moo-moo"

*Continue with other animals
and their sounds.*

THIS LITTLE PIGGY

Help Children:
- **Become familiar with toes/fingers.**
- **Play with voices.**

FIND YOUR PIGS

Take off your shoes and/or socks and find your *pigs*. (A good time to do this is when your children naturally have their shoes/socks off, such as nap time.) As you are all saying the fingerplay touch your toes. Say it again touching the toes on the same or other foot.

THIS LITTLE PIGGY/TOE*

This little piggy/toe went to market.
  (*Touch big toe.*)
This little piggy/toe stayed home.
  (*Touch toe.*)
This little piggy/toe had roast beef.
  (*Touch toe.*)
This little piggy/toe had none.
  (*Touch toe.*)
This little piggy/toe cried,
  (*Touch small toe.*)
"Wee, wee, wee, wee, wee" all the way home.

*Use the word **toe** if your children are not familiar with their toes. If they regularly use the word toe, using the word **piggy** is fun. You decide which is most appropriate for your children.*

THIS LITTLE FINGER

Instead of talking about and touching toes, change the word toe to finger. Begin with your thumb and move to your fingers as you say the new fingerplay.

This little finger went to market.
This little finger stayed home.
This little finger had roast beef.
This little finger had none.
This little finger cried,
"Wee, wee, wee, wee, wee" all the way home.

WALK OLD JOE

Help Children:
- Move in different ways.
- Cooperate.
- Develop sense of touch.

MUSICAL CHAIRS
Collect a variety of floor mats, pillows, cushions, small rugs, etc. at least one for each child. Put them in a circle. Pretend you're *"Old Joe"* and walk around the circle saying the rhyme. At the last line, stop, fall down on the mat near you and kick up your legs. Stand up and play again.

IN THE STABLE
Get several plastic milk bottles. Wash them out. Near the bottom of each one, cut a large door. Put toy horses in bottles. Set them on the floor for children to play with.

WALK OLD JOE

Walk old Joe
   (Tap hands on floor.)
Walk old Joe
You're the best horse
   in the country
Walk old Joe
Walk old Joe
Whoa Joe!
   (Lay back and kick your legs)

   Trot ...

   Gallop ...

BEAR WENT OVER

WHAT DID HE SEE?
Gather up 6-8 small toys that your children like to play with. Put them in a box.

OR

Cut out large pictures of things that your children are familiar with and glue each one to piece of construction paper.

Have the toys/pictures handy. Sing the first verse of the song with the children. Continue singing, *"And all that he could see was..."* At this point stop and hold up a toy or picture. Everyone call out what the bear saw and clap for him. Sing and play again and again.

THE BEAR WENT OVER THE MOUNTAIN

The bear went over the mountain,
*(Bend arm and walk fingers
up to the elbow.)*
The bear went over the mountain,
The bear went over the mountain,
To see what he could see.

And all that he could see,
And all that he could see,

Was the other side of the mountain
The other side of the mountain,
The other side of the mountain
Was all that he could see.

FIVE MONKEYS JUMPING

Help Children:
- **Become aware of numbers.**
- **Be safe.**
- **Call doctors.**

USE YOUR GLOVE
Duplicate, cut out, and add a piece of Velcro® to the five small monkeys and then attach them to your Velcro® glove. As you say the rhyme, have the appropriate number of monkeys jumping around.

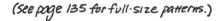
(See page 135 for full-size patterns.)

FIVE LITTLE MONKEYS JUMPING ON THE BED

Five little monkeys jumping on the bed.
(Hold up 5 fingers.)
One fell off and bumped his head.
Mama called the doctor,
And the doctor said,
(Say firmly.)
"No more monkeys jumping on the bed!"
(Shake head 'no'.)

Four little monkeys jumping...

Three little monkeys jumping...

Two little monkeys jumping...

One little monkey jumping...

FIVE MONKEYS SWINGING

* **Become aware of numbers.**
* **Use whisper voices.**
* **Anticipate.**
* **Wait.**

MR ALLIGATOR

Get a green sock. (Add simple alligator features if you'd like.) Slip it on your arm so that the toe fits over your hand.

Keep the alligator behind your back as everyone starts to sing and then let it quietly swim towards the monkeys. Open its mouth and SNAP! Quietly swim back behind your back.

VARIATION: When the alligator *"snaps"* squeeze several children's fingers at each verse.

USE YOUR GLOVE

Duplicate the five monkey patterns on page 109. Put them on your Velcro® glove and say the rhyme.

FIVE LITTLE MONKEYS SWINGING IN THE TREE

Five little monkeys swinging in the tree.
   (Hold up 5 fingers.)
Teasing Mr. Alligator,
   (Swing fingers back and forth.)
"Can't catch me!"
"Can't catch me!"

Along came Mr Alligator
   (Whisper voice.)
As quietly as can be
SNAP!
   (Clap hands loudly.)

Four little monkeys swinging......
Three little monkeys swinging......
Two little monkeys swinging......
One little monkey swinging......

I'M A LION

Help Children:
- **Name animals.**
- **Sound like animals.**
- **Anticipate.**

STICK PUPPET FUN
Find pictures of animals or enlarge and duplicate these. Make a stick puppet for each animal. As you name each animal hold up the puppet.

see pages 136 & 137 for full-size patterns.)

I'M A LION

Adult: *I'm a lion. Hear me...*
Children: Make lion sound.

Adult: *I'm a bear. Hear me...*
Children: Make bear sound.

Adult: *I'm a snake. Hear me...*
Children: Make snake sound.

Adult: *I'm a monkey. Hear me...*
Children: Make monkey sound.

FROGGIE IN THE MIDDLE

Help Children:
- **Socialize.**
- **Play group games.**
- **Jump.**
- **Take turns.**

JUMP! JUMP!
Use a small trampoline. (If you do not have an individual trampoline, use a small tumbling mat.) Put the trampoline in an open area. Stand, holding hands in a circle around it. Name a child to be the *froggie in the middle*. She jumps on the trampoline while everyone sings. Clap at the end. Name another child to be the next *froggie* and continue singing and playing.

HINT: Stand next to the children as they jump on the trampoline.

FROGGIE IN THE MIDDLE

There's a froggie in the middle
　(Child jumps.)
And he can't get out,
He can't get out,
He can't get out.

There's a froggie in the middle
And he can't get out,
(Name child) lend him a hand
　(Hold hands.)
And help him out.
　(Walk out together.)

FLUFFY

Help Children:
- **Learn body parts.**

HERE COMES FLUFFY
Get a small stuffed bunny or rabbit puppet. Put it in an empty tissue box which has an opening on the top.

Bring the *secret box* to show the children. Cover up the opening. Guess what might be inside. Bring *Fluffy* out of the box and say the fingerplay with the children. Let *Fluffy* do the movements with the children.

FLUFFY

Fluffy the bunny is,
Fat, fat, fat.
  (Stick out tummy.)
His soft little paws go,
Pat, pat, pat.
  (Tap feet.)

His soft little ears go,
Flop, flop, flop.
  (Hands by ears.)
His strong little legs go,
Hop, hop, hop.
  (Jump.)

FUNNY BUNNY

Help Children:
- **Coordinate both hands.**
- **Exercise their whole body.**
- **Jump.**

FUNNY BUNNY

Get a light-colored, wooly winter glove. Using a permanent marker, draw a bunny face on it. Say the rhyme with the children using the *"funny bunny"* puppet.

JUMPED INTO HIS HOLE

Using a clothesline, form a big circle (hole) in an open area of the room. Stand around the outside of the bunny hole and pretend that you are funny bunnies as you hop all around. After hopping for a little while say to the bunnies, *"Stop!* (Pause.) *I hear a noise! Get back in your hole."* All of the bunnies jump into the hole and cover up their heads. Clap!

FUNNY BUNNY

Here is a bunny
(Bend index and middle finger on one hand.)

With ears so funny.

Here is his hole in the ground.
(Make a circle with other hand.)

He hears a noise and perks up his ears.
(Straighten index and middle fingers.)

He jumps into his hole in the ground.
("Ears" jump into circle.)

"GUNK, GUNK"

Help Children:
- **Exercise.**
- **Identify body parts.**

FROG EXERCISE
Get a frog puppet or a green sock and let the frog lead the children in exercises. Everyone follow the puppet and sing, *Gunk, Gunk* together.

Expand the song by keeping the first three lines the same and changing the last line. As you sing the last line, do the action with the frog.

For example:

- *"And his legs went jump, jump, jump."*
- *"And his knees went wiggle, wiggle, wiggle."*
- *"And his arms went round, round, round."*
- *"And his waist bent up and down."*

"GUNK, GUNK" WENT THE LITTLE GREEN FROG

"Gunk, gunk" went
    the little green frog one day.
    (Accent "Gunk, gunk.")

"Gunk, gunk" went
    the little green frog.

"Gunk, gunk" went
    the little green frog one day.

And his eyes went
    "Blink, blink, blink."
    (Open and close eyes.)

LITTLE TURTLE

Help Children:
- Learn to sequence.
- Control rhythm sticks.

SNAP
Pass out rhythm sticks and have the children hold them in their laps. Slowly say the second verse, stretch your arms out and *snap* your sticks together as the turtle snaps at the mosquito, flea, minnow, and child.

LITTLE TURTLE

There was a little turtle
  (Cup hands.)
Who lived in a box.
He swam in a pond.
He climbed on the rocks.

He snapped at a mosquito.
  (Clap hands.)
He snapped at a flea.
He snapped at a minnow.
He snapped at me.

He caught that mosquito.
  (Grab air with hands.)
He caught that flea.
He caught that minnow.
But he didn't catch me.

RUN, RUN, RABBIT

Help Children:
- **Combine rhythm and words.**
- **Control rhythm sticks.**
- **Use energy.**

GATHER AT THE TABLE
Stand at one of your larger tables. Begin to slowly say the rhyme, while looking around the room and encouraging the children to come and stand at the table. Have the children say the rhyme with you. When you all say, *"Run, run, rabbit..."* slap the top of the table instead of your thighs. At the end everyone clap.

RHYTHM STICK TAP
Sit on the floor. Give each child rhythm sticks. Say the rhyme together. When you say *"Run, run, rabbit..."* keep the beat by tapping your rhythm sticks on the floor.

RUN, RUN, RABBIT

There once was a fox
    (Slowly, with inflection.)
A sly silver fox.
Who was always
Looking for a rabbit.
    (Hands above eyes looking for a fox.)

Run, run, rabbit.
    (Say quickly and slap thighs.)
Run, run, rabbit.
Run, run, rabbit.
As fast as you can.

Don't let him catch me.
    (Hug yourself.)
Don't let him catch me.
Don't let him put me,
In that rabbit stew.

    Repeat the second and third verses faster.

And he did.
Yes, he did!
That little rabbit ran so fast,
He got away!
    (Clap.)

TWO LITTLE BLACKBIRDS

Help Children:
- **Follow directions.**
- **Control rhythm sticks.**
- **Learn opposites.**

FLY AWAY

After the children have enjoyed the rhyme using their thumbs for Jack and Jill, give each child a pair of rhythm sticks or tongue depressors. Let the children pretend that their *sticks* are Jack and Jill. Say the first verse of the rhyme using the *sticks*. Extend the rhyme by changing the words and actions of the fourth, fifth, sixth, and seventh lines. Inflection is very important as you accent the opposite words each time.

- Fly away <u>low</u>, fly away <u>high</u>.
- Fly away <u>slow</u>, fly away <u>fast</u>.
- Fly away <u>quiet</u>, fly away <u>loud</u>.
- Fly away <u>straight</u>, fly away <u>wiggly</u>.

Continue with other opposites.

TWO LITTLE BLACKBIRDS

Two little blackbirds
Sitting on the hill.
  (Make fists.)
One named Jack, one named Jill.
  (Raise one thumb, then other.)
Fly away Jack.
  (Fly one thumb behind back.)
Fly away Jill.
  (Fly other thumb behind back.)
Come back Jack.
  (Fly one thumb back.)
Come back Jill.
  (Fly other thumb back.)

TEN LITTLE BIRDIES

Help Children:
- Move creatively.
- Count.
- Be aware of nature.

FLY AROUND

Fly around as you sing *Ten Little Birdies* over and over again. Remember to clap often.

BIRD HUNT

On a nice day take a slow walk around your neighborhood. Look for birds sitting on the ground, flying in the sky, searching for food, resting in the trees, perched on wires, etc.

EXTENSION: Hang a bird feeder near one of your windows. Watch the birds throughout the day.

TEN LITTLE BIRDIES

1 little, 2 little, 3 little birdies,

4 little, 5 little, 6 little birdies,

7 little, 8 little, 9 little birdies,

10 little flying birds.

Help Children:
- Move creatively.
- Count.
- Be aware of nature.

FLY AROUND
Fly around the room like Ten Little Birdies over...

BIRD HUNT
On a nice day take a slow walk around your neighborhood. Look for birds sitting on the ground, flying in the sky, perching in trees...

TEN LITTLE BIRDIES

Bugs & Insects

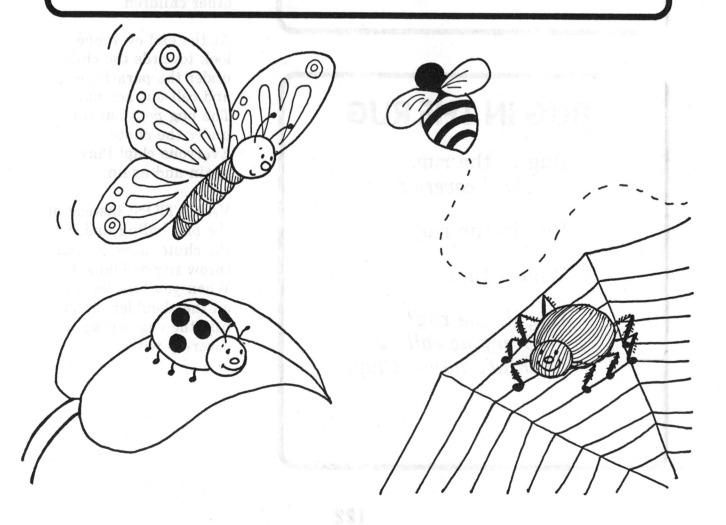

BUG IN THE RUG

Help Children:
- Learn names.
- Sit quietly.
- Play with a group.

PEEK-A-BOO
Everyone sit around a parachute, blanket, or bedsheet. Walk around the circle. Stop and tap a child on the shoulder. That child pulls the parachute over her head. Sit down next to the child and say *Bug In The Rug* with the other children.

At the end everyone look towards the child under the parachute and call out her name. The bug *pops* out from under the chute. Everyone clap! Play again and again.

VARIATION: Instead of the *bug* hiding under the chute, have a small throw rug or blanket. When you tap the child on the shoulder, hand him the rug/blanket to cover-up with.

BUG IN THE RUG

Bug in the rug.
   (Child covers face.)

Bug in the rug.

Who is that

Bug in the rug?
   (Everyone call out child's name. Clap)

122

EENSY-WEENSY SPIDER

Help Children:
- Play with their voices.
- Coordinate finger movements.
- Add sound variations to their vocabulary.

EENSY-WEENSY SPIDERS
Pretend to be eensy-weensy spiders. As you all whisper the first verse, walk quietly in place. Sprinkle *rain* on all of the spiders and have them fall down. Make your arms into a circle and walk around drying up the rain. As you do, the spiders get up and walk quietly again. Quietly clap for the spiders. Play again!

VARIATION: Play *Great Big Giant Spider*. See page 124.

EENSY-WEENSY SPIDER

The eensy-weensy spider
Walked up the water spout.
   (Walk fingers up arm.)

Down came the rain
   (Flick your fingers overhead.)
And washed the spider out.

Out came the sun
   (Big circle overhead.)
And dried up all the rain.

And the eensy-weensy spider
   (Walk fingers up arm.)
Walked up the spout again.

Help Children:
- **Play with their voices.**
- **Add sound variations to their vocabulary.**

GIANT SPIDERS

Pretend to be *giant spiders* walking in place. In loud, deep voices begin to say the rhyme. Sprinkle *rain* on the spiders and make them fall down. Make your arms into a circle and walk around drying up the rain. As you do, the giant spiders get up and walk in place again. Clap loudly for the spiders. Play again.

VARIATION: Play *Eensy-Weensy Spider*. See page 123.

GREAT BIG GIANT SPIDER

The great big giant spider
Walked up the water spout.
   (Walk fingers in giant steps up arm.)

Down came the rain.
   (Flick fingers overhead.)
And washed the spider out.

Out came the sun.
   (Big circle overhead.)
And dried up all the rain.

And the great big giant spider
   (Giant steps up arm.)
Walked up the spout again.

HERE IS THE BEEHIVE

Help Children:
- **Become aware of numbers.**
- **Understand opposites.**
- **Learn the bee's buzzing sound.**

BUZZING AROUND
Say the rhyme together while doing the actions. At the end, pretend you're bees flying around the room making buzzing sounds.

VARIATIONS:
- Be quiet bees, buzzing softly.
- Be noisy bees, buzzing loudly.
- Slow bees, moving slowly.
- Fast bees, flying quickly.

USE YOUR GLOVE:
Duplicate 5 small bees and attach them to your Velcro® glove. When you count the bees at the end of the rhyme, raise each finger slowly as you let each bee out of the hive.

(See page 138 for full-sized bee patterns.)

HERE IS THE BEEHIVE

Here is the beehive.
   (Close fist.)
Where are the bees?
   (Look at fist.)
Hidden away
      where nobody sees.

Here they come creeping
Out of the hive.
1, 2, 3, 4, 5.
   (Open fist, one finger at a time.)

BABY BUMBLE BEE

- **Name different body parts.**
- **Learn bee safety.**

OUCH HE STUNG ME
Before you begin singing *Bumble Bee*, pretend to grab a bee from the air and hold it in your cupped hands. Sing the song. At the end, quickly go around to each child and *sting* him with your pointer finger. As you *sting* each child, name the body part you are touching.

VARIATION: Let the children tell you where to *sting* them.

BUMBLE BEE

I'm bringing home
   (*Hands clasped, swinging*
   back and forth.)
My baby bumble bee.
Won't my mommy
   be so proud of me.
I'm bringing home
   my baby bumble bee.
Ouch!
He stung me!
Yes siree!

BEE SAFETY
Sing *I'm Walking Away* with the children. Talk about bee safety.

I'm walking away
From the bumble bee.
Won't my mommy
Be so proud of me.
I'm walking away
From the bumble bee.
He didn't sting me,
No siree!
   (Shake head no.)

THERE'S A BUG ON ME

Help Children
- **Become aware of numbers.**
- **Name body parts.**
- **Learn position words.**

WHERE'S THE BUG?
Get a plastic bug. Hide it in your hand. Say the fingerplay with the children. As you're saying the last line, quietly set the bug someplace on your body and then say to the children, *"Look for the bug!"* The children should look all around your body until they find it, and then call out where it is.

VARIATION: Get a big leaf from the yard or cut a large construction paper leaf. Hide the bug *near the leaf -- next to, under, on top of, in the middle, on the edge, etc.*

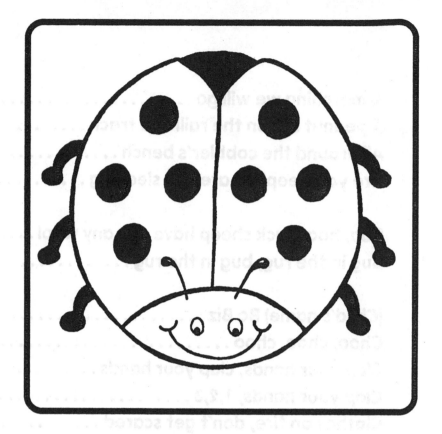

1, 2, 3 THERE'S A BUG ON ME

1,2,3 there's a bug on me.
(Hold up fingers.)

Where did he go?

I don't know.
(Shrug your shoulders.)

Appendix

LITTLE CLOWNS

(Use clown patterns with: •*Little Clowns*, p. 37 •*This Little Clown*, p. 40)

132

USE YOUR EYES

(Use clothing patterns with: •*Use Your Eyes*, p. 62.)

OLD MacDONALD

(Use farm animal patterns with: •*Old MacDonald*, p. 105.)

FIVE MONKEYS JUMPING

(Use monkey patterns with: •*Five Monkeys Jumping*, p. 109 •*Five Monkeys Swinging*, p. 110)

I'M A LION, p.1

(Use animal patterns with: •*I'm A Lion*, p. 111.)

(Use animal patterns with: •*I'm A Lion*, p. 111.)

FIVE LITTLE DUCKS / HERE IS THE BEEHIVE

(Use duck patterns with: •*Five Little Ducks*, p. 101 •*Five Little Ducks Play*, p. 102.
Use bee patterns with: •*Here Is The Beehive*, p. 125.)

Building Blocks Library

The Circle Time Series

by Liz and Dick Wilmes. Hundreds of activities for large and small groups of children. Each book is filled with Language and Active games, Fingerplays, Songs, Stories, Snacks, and more. A great resource for every library shelf.

Circle Time Book
Captures the spirit of 39 holidays and seasons.
ISBN 0-943452-00-7   **$ 12.95**

Everyday Circle Times
Over 900 ideas. Choose from 48 topics divided into 7 sections: self-concept, basic concepts, animals, foods, science, occupations, and recreation.
ISBN 0-943452-01-5   **$16.95**

More Everyday Circle Times
Divided into the same 7 sections as EVERYDAY. Features new topics such as Birds and Pizza, plus all new ideas for some popular topics contained in EVERYDAY.
ISBN 0-943452-14-7   **$16.95**

Yearful of Circle Times
52 different topics to use weekly, by seasons, or mixed throughout the year. New Friends, Signs of Fall, Snowfolk Fun, and much more.
ISBN 0-943452-10-4   **$16.95**

Paint Without Brushes

by Liz and Dick Wilmes. Use common materials which you already have. Discover the painting possibilities in your classroom! PAINT WITHOUT BRUSHES gives your children open-ended art activities to explore paint in lots of creative ways. A valuable art resource. One you'll want to use daily.
ISBN 0-943452-15-5   **$12.95**

Easel Art

by Liz & Dick Wilmes. Let the children use easels, walls, outside fences, clip boards, and more as they enjoy the variety of art activities filling the pages of EASEL ART. A great book to expand young children's art experiences.
ISBN 0-943452-25-2   **$ 12.95**

Everyday Bulletin Boards

by Wilmes and Moehling. Features borders, murals, backgrounds, and other open-ended art to display on your bulletin boards. Plus board ideas with patterns, which teachers can make and use to enhance their curriculum.
ISBN 0-943452-09-0   **$ 12.95**

Exploring Art

by Liz and Dick Wilmes. EXPLORING ART is divided by months. Over 250 art ideas for paint, chalk, doughs, scissors, and more. Easy to set-up in your classroom.
ISBN 0-943452-05-8   **$19.95**

Parachute Play

by Liz and Dick Wilmes. A year 'round approach to one of the most versatile pieces of large muscle equipment. Starting with basic techniques, PARACHUTE PLAY provides over 100 activities to use with your parachute.
ISBN 0-943452-03-1 **$ 9.95**

Learning Centers

by Liz and Dick Wilmes. Hundreds of open-ended activities to quickly involve and excite your children. You'll use it every time you plan and whenever you need a quick, additional activity. A must for every teacher's bookshelf.
ISBN 0-943452-13-9 **$19.95**

Play With Big Boxes

by Liz and Dick Wilmes. Children love big boxes. Turn them into boats, telephone booths, tents, and other play areas. Bring them to art and let children collage, build, and paint them. Use them in learning centers for games, walk-along vehicles, play stages, quiet spaces, puzzles, and more, more, more.
ISBN 0-943452-23-6 **$ 12.95**

Play With Small Boxes

by Liz and Dick Wilmes. Small boxes are free, fun, and provide unlimited possibilities. Use them for telephones, skates, scoops, pails, beds, buggies, and more. So many easy activities, you'll want to use small boxes every day.
ISBN 0-943452-24-4 **$ 12.95**

Felt Board Fingerplays

by Liz and Dick Wilmes. Over fifty popular fingerplays, each with full-size patterns. All accompanied by games and activities to extend the learning and play even more. Divided by seasons, this book is a quick reference for a year full of fingerplay fun.
ISBN 0-943452-26-0 **$16.95**

Felt Board Fun

by Liz and Dick Wilmes. Make your felt board come alive. Discover how versatile it is as the children become involved with a wide range of activities. This unique book has over 150 ideas with accompanying patterns.
ISBN 0-943452-02-3 **$16.95**

Table & Floor Games

by Liz and Dick Wilmes. 32 easy-to-make, fun-to-play table/floor games with accompanying patterns ready to trace or photocopy. Teach beginning concepts such as matching, counting, colors, alphabet, sorting and so on.
ISBN 0-943452-16-3 **$19.95**

Activities Unlimited

by Adler, Caton, and Cleveland. Create an enthusiasm for learning! Hundreds of innovative activities to help your children develop fine and gross motor skills, increase their language, become self-reliant, and play cooperatively. Whether you're a beginning teacher or a veteran, this book will quickly become one of your favorites.
ISBN 0-943452-17-1 **$16.95**

2's Experience Series

by Liz and Dick Wilmes. An exciting series developed especially for toddlers and twos!

2's Experience - Art
Scribble, Paint, Smear, Mix , Tear, Mold, Taste, and more. Over 150 activities, plus lots of recipes and hints.
ISBN 0-943452-21-X   **$16.95**

2's Experience - Dramatic Play
Dress up and pretend! Hundreds of imaginary characters... fire-fighters, campers, bus drivers, and more.
ISBN 0-943452-20-1   **$12.95**

2's Experience - Felt Board Fun
Make your felt board come alive. Enjoy stories, activities, and rhymes developed just for very young children. Hundreds of patterns feature teddy bears, and much, much more.
     $14.95

Fingerplays
fingerplays with large FINGERPLAY CARDS.
     $12.95

Sensory Play
multi-sensory activities to encourage look, listen, taste, touch, and smell.
943452-22-8   **$14.95**

TODDLERS & TWO'S

BUILDING BLOCKS Subscription	$20.00
2's EXPERIENCE Series	
2'S EXPERIENCE - ART	16.95
2'S EXPERIENCE - DRAMATIC PLAY	12.95
2'S EXPERIENCE - FELTBOARD FUN	14.95
2'S EXPERIENCE - FINGERPLAYS	12.95
2'S EXPERIENCE - SENSORY PLAY	14.95
CIRCLE TIME Series	
CIRCLE TIME BOOK	12.95
EVERYDAY CIRCLE TIMES	16.95
MORE EVERYDAY CIRCLE TIMES	16.95
YEARFUL OF CIRCLE TIMES	16.95
ART	
EASEL ART	12.95
EVERYDAY BULLETIN BOARDS	12.95
EXPLORING ART	19.95
PAINT WITHOUT BRUSHES	12.95
LEARNING GAMES & ACTIVITIES	
ACTIVITIES UNLIMITED	16.95
FELT BOARD FINGERPLAYS	16.95
FELT BOARD FUN	16.95
LEARNING CENTERS	19.95
PARACHUTE PLAY	9.95
PLAY WITH BIG BOXES	12.95
PLAY WITH SMALL BOXES	12.95
TABLE & FLOOR GAMES	19.95

Prices subject to change without notice.

All books available from full-service book stores, educational stores, and school supply catalogs.